ask me
where I'm going

& other revealing messages from  TODAY'S TEENS

"Ask Me Where I'm Going" and
Other Revealing Messages from Today's Teens

Copyright © 2004 Search Institute

Adapted from the poster set *In Our Own Words* (Copyright © 2000 Search Institute)
developed by Kathryn (Kay) L. Hong

ISBN: 1-57482-854-1

Search Institute
615 First Avenue Northeast, Suite 125
Minneapolis, MN 55413
612-376-8955
800-888-7828
www.search-institute.org

Credits
Editor: Ruth Taswell
Design: Jeanne Lee
Production: Mary Ellen Buscher

To Tim, Molly, Mike, Josh, Rachel, Lemmy, LaTesha, James, Nathan, Sarah, Chelsi, Tony, Hunter, Christy, Mike, Jeremy, and Sara, who contributed their thoughts on what they really want from adults in their lives.

Do you remember what it felt like to be a teenager?

EAGER FOR FREEDOM, YET IN NEED OF GUIDANCE, TOO?
Wanting encouragement to grow and to try
new things, but also wanting to be included and
accepted just for being you?

FOR TEENS TODAY, MUCH OF WHAT THEY DESIRE IN LIFE
is no different. Although they seem to face many
more difficult choices than teens of previous
generations, the need to know that someone
cares about who they are and what they hope for
remains the same. Knowing someone really
cares can make all their dreams, big and small,
feel possible.

GIVEN TODAY'S COMPLEX WORLD, JUST *HOW* CAN YOU
show a teenager you care? As adults, we so easily
rally around babies and young children. But with

teens, we often hold our breath, hoping they'll make it through the teen years safe and sound or waiting until they do something wrong. To help teens grow into healthy, caring, responsible people, adults need to rally around teens as well. We need to listen to what teens want adults to hear.

IN THE PAGES THAT FOLLOW, REAL TEENS TELL YOU WHAT they want and need from any adult in their lives—not just parents or teachers. You *can* make an important difference in teens' lives; it doesn't matter whether they are your own kids, relatives, neighbors, or strangers walking down the street.

THINK ABOUT WHAT THEY HAVE TO SAY. WHAT THEY HOPE for—and deserve—is possible and necessary. As you read their words, you'll realize how simple, wise, and realistic their requests are.

[support]

BE THE FIRST *to smile or wave when we pass by one another.*

Get to know me.

LET ME SHARE MY WORRIES WITH YOU.

Talk with me.

let

ACCEPT ME

Let me trust you with my secrets.

FOR WHO I AM.

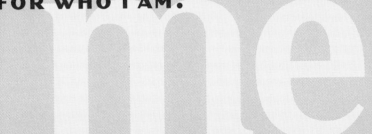

SHOW ME *you care about my schoolwork by coming to my teacher conferences —*

even though I don't really like having those conferences or you being there!

ENCOURAGE ME MORE,

CRITICIZE ME LESS—

AT HOME AND AT SCHOOL.

Don't yell at me
for making mistakes.

you

DON'T GET MAD

STAND UP FOR ME.

with

WHEN I MESS UP.

my se

TRY TO UNDERSTAND ME.

DO THINGS WITH ME.

crets

NEVER GIVE UP
ON ME.

Love me.

[empowerment]

Give me a voice.

TAKE ME SERIOUSLY.

Acknowledge my opinions.

TREAT ME LIKE AN EQUAL.

ACCEPT AND

Teach by example.

UNDERSTAND **MY MISTAKES.**

APPLAUD
**MY EFFORTS AND
SUCCESSES.**

my

Help me SOLVE PROBLEMS
and change things for the better.

LET ME TAKE CARE OF THINGS

efforts

Trust me.

WHEN I THINK I CAN.

LET ME MAKE
MY OWN
DECISIONS.

and

Let me still be a child sometimes.

Give me ideas
and feedback.

SUC

REMEMBER

THAT SOMEDAY SOON

I WILL BE

COMPLETELY IN CHARGE

OF MY LIFE.

[boundaries & expectations]

Don't expect me to fail.

Comfort me
when I do.

HELP ME

LEARN

ABOUT THE WORLD.

Challenge me to succeed.

But don't expect **TOO MUCH** —
I can feel
like a failure
and give up.

ask

BE AWARE.

Be concerned.

me

BE SUPPORTIVE.

where

ASK M

I'm

Watch out for my safety.

WHERE **I'M GOING.**

SET FAIR
BOUNDARIES.

BE WILLING TO

going

Apply standards consistently.

NEGOTIATE NEW RULES **WITH ME.**

Help me grow to be an individual.

EXPECT ME
TO DO MY BEST.

[constructive use of time]

Invite me.
INSPIRE ME.

DON'T CAGE ME

OR SUPPRESS ME.

*Don't cram my time with pointless
and boring activities.*

don't

OPEN UP MORE PLACES TO GO.

LET ME
HAVE TIME FOR
FREEDOM.

cage

Notice
when I do useful things.

or sup

TRY TO UNDERSTAND

THE WAY I THINK

ABOUT SPIRITUAL AND

RELIGIOUS IDEAS.

LET ME PLAY.

Let me dream.

[commitment to learning]

GIVE ME A CHANCE—

AND A BREAK

EVERY ONCE IN A WHILE.

Welcome me.

pay

HELP ME TREAT SCHOOL AS I

Introduce me to a NEW AUTHOR.

T IS MY JOB.

Make school less like a factory and more like a community.

atten

KEEP CLASSES SMALL.
KEEP HALLWAYS FRIENDLY.

Be excited
about your subject.

Be sincere.

to

TREAT MI

me

LIKE A HUMAN BEING.

PAY ATTENTION
TO ME.

Feed my interests.

RESPECT MY CHOICES.
Respect me.

[positive values]

Be honest with yourself.

**BE HONEST
WITH ME.**

[positive values]

Help me act from my ideals.

LISTEN **WHEN I TALK ABOUT TH**

THINGS THAT MEAN SOMETHING TO ME.

Help me be responsible when I experiment with new activities.

REMIND ME

THAT IF I START USING

ALCOHOL

OR OTHER DRUGS,

IT CAN BE REALLY HARD

TO STOP.

honest

Have the courage to tell me
or someone else you're sorry.

with me

ACCEPT ME,
NO MATTER HOW
"DIFFERENT"
I AM FROM YOU.

[social competencies]

SHOW ME HOW TO

TURN STRANGERS INTO

FRIENDS.

TEACH ME *acceptance and respect, and I won't have to learn tolerance.*

Have all different
kinds of friends —
male and female,
of different religions and
different races.

be a

GIVE ME THE CHANCE TO BE "COOL," TO BE RECOGNIZED AS A BEAUTIFUL INDIVIDUAL, NO MATTER HOW I LOOK.

good

[social competencies]

role

CONSIDER ME A PERSON

BE A GOOD
ROLE MODEL.

Be the one who speaks out for peace.

model
OT SOMETHING TO BE LABELED.

[positive identity]

REMIND ME
THAT I'M
WORTHWHILE.

*Encourage me to give tough things
my best shot.*

Help me find my talents.

help

REASSURE ME

HELP ME
BE REALISTIC.

WHEN I'M HAVING DOUBTS.

me

GIVE M

Don't be a **HYPOCRITE** —
you were young once, too.

SINCERE COMPLIMENTS.

find

Be kind to me.

BELIEVE
THAT I CAN DO
GOOD THINGS
FOR THE WORLD.

my

Tell me what's good about me.

ta

REMEMBER THERE IS NO

Help me
learn to be happy
with myself.

ents

PERFECT PERSON OUT THERE.

CELEBRATE
MY UNIQUENESS.

Like me just for who I am.

Search Institute

Powerful evidence shows that what teenagers *want* is also what teenagers *need*. Research indicates that through positive relationships with caring adults, teens can develop the skills, values, and self-perceptions they need to grow up and become strong, resilient, happy adults.

Over the years, Search Institute has identified these relationships, skills, and values as "developmental assets" that all children need to succeed. These assets (spread across eight broad areas of human development) are about individual capacity, not financial worth. They're about striving to make a difference in the lives of kids.

All adults can give teenagers what they need—and what they're asking for—by building these eight areas of developmental assets for and with them. **The first four areas** focus on the *external* relationships and opportunities you can create for teenagers:

♥ **SUPPORT** Teens need to be surrounded by adults who love, care about, appreciate, accept, and include them. Teens need to know that they belong and that they are not alone.

EMPOWERMENT Teens need to feel that adults believe that they have something to contribute and are allowed to do so. Being empowered—knowing that you are valued and valuable—means feeling safe, liked and respected, and confident to explore dreams and opportunities.

✪ **BOUNDARIES AND EXPECTATIONS** Teens need the positive influence of adults who encourage them to be and do their best. Teens also need to know that what adults expect of them is reasonable, clear, and consistent, and that adults believe teens can meet high expectations.

CONSTRUCTIVE USE OF TIME Teens need lots of opportunities to explore who they are and where they fit in—to find activities and learn new skills that satisfy different aspects of themselves: their physical selves, their spiritual, social, and emotional sides, and their minds.

The next four categories reflect the abilities, values, attitudes, and commitments that teenagers, with your help, develop *internally*.

COMMITMENT TO LEARNING Teens need to link learning to more than just school. They need a wide variety of learning experiences. A desire for success—and not just for the good grades—can also mean believing in their own abilities and having a sense of the lasting importance of learning.

POSITIVE VALUES Teens need strong, guiding principles to develop the confidence to make decisions on their own without feeling they have to follow the crowd. Teens need to learn to stand up for themselves and for others.

SOCIAL COMPETENCIES Teens need to learn to understand how others might feel and to respect them even if they disagree. Being a caring friend, coping with new situations, and making difficult decisions are all key for teens to feel good about themselves and comfortable around others.

POSITIVE IDENTITY Teens need to believe in their own self-worth, in their ability to make good things happen. If teens feel that they have control over the things that happen to them, they're more likely to have a sense of purpose in life as well as feel hopeful about the future.

HEAR WHAT TEENS WANT TO TELL YOU,

wherever they are in your life.

SUPPORT AND ACCEPT THEM for who they are.

LET THEM KNOW you believe in their abilities.

ENCOURAGE THEM to be their best.

INSPIRE THEM to spend their time well.

PROVIDE THEM with opportunities to learn new things that feel meaningful to them.

PROMOTE VALUES that are worthy of upholding.

HELP THEM understand how to make good choices.

BE HOPEFUL about their future.

You can give teens the love and guidance they need and deserve.

Search Institute is an independent, nonprofit, nonsectarian research and education organization whose mission is to provide leadership, knowledge, and resources to promote healthy children, youth, and communities. The institute collaborates with others to promote long-term organizational and cultural change that supports its mission. For a free information packet, call **800-888-7828** or visit our Web site at **www.search-institute.org**.